LEGIT AND QUICK WAYS TO MAKE MONEY ONLINE WITHOUT MONEY.

Your first $1000 guaranteed!

LEGIT AND QUICK WAYS TO MAKE MONEY ONLINE WITHOUT MONEY.

YOUR FIRST $1000 GUARANTEED!

"Create a life where you can be financially free"

WRITTEN BY

Ibe Okechukwu

TABLE OF CONTENTS

Introduction

Welcome to “Legit and quick ways to make money online without money
Your first $1000 guaranteed!"

This ebook is here to be a guide and to help get you on the right track to making money online.

I'm giving you access to these tried-and-true internet income options. Along with many of my students, I have personally used these strategies to MAKE LEGIT AND QUICK MONEY ONLINE. Just keep in mind that nothing worthwhile is free. You must be prepared to give it your all!

If you make the decision to stick with it, you will succeed! Many people give up just as their breakthrough occurs. You can achieve success if you set a goal, create an action plan, and follow the steps.

Please let me know when you make your first sale from this ebook! The success stories that keep coming in from all around the world never get old to me. Your moment to shine has come!

Happy earning!
Ibe Okechukwu

CHAPTER 1

(1) Become an online assistant

There is a good opportunity to find a full-time position as a virtual assistant because all organizations require assistance with managing their routine administrative work. This form of remote employment will. provide you flexibility and ensure that you never grow bored because virtual assistants deal with a variety of activities. You might as well start right away if you have a phone, an internet connection, a Skype account, and some office expertise.

(2) **Promote your design**

You can easily start selling your own designs if you are skilled at designing and producing distinctive graphics. There are several websites out there that provide you the chance to sell your design as T-shirts, purses, mugs, etc. Keep your creations printable as the sole thing to be on the lookout for. You will start getting a commission for each item that is sold once your ideas start to become popular. The only thing you will be required to do is input your photographs. Shipping or printing the design are not issues. There are normally no expenses associated with registration, but you should start considering your own brand before you begin. It always turns out to be a wise choice. Coming up with a memorable name at least always turns out to be a terrific idea, as people can follow your business and will keep an eye on your work. You may boost your reputation and increase sales by developing your own brand and selling original artworks.

(3) Earn from ebooks and information products

You're looking at the ideal instance of how to MAKE MONEY FROM BOOKS! Online users have a voracious need for knowledge. One of the easiest methods to start earning money online and establishing yourself as an authority is to package your expertise. In truth, you don't even need to be an expert. People can be readily directed to the appropriate sources of knowledge, including links to and references to the work of other authorities. You can resell my professional insights after buying this ebook, and other people would appreciate it if you do. This ebook is not a private label product; rather, it is a product where someone else has produced the material and you have the right to repackage it under your name or brand. How simple was that? Using a private label product eliminates the need for you to even write it yourself. PLR PRODUCTS are available in many locations. There are a ton of PLR products if you just Google them! They are also available in bulk purchases. Before you put your name on anything, just make sure the content is of high quality! If you're repackaging PLR products or writing your own ebooks... Links to AFFILIATE PRODUCTS you advocate or that will enhance the knowledge you are sharing should be included. You may increase your earning potential and aid your customer in obtaining the best products to help them achieve their goals by introducing links to affiliate products. Google Docs is a useful tool for working through your content when it comes to PACKAGING YOUR EBOOK.

Then, all you have to do is select File, Download as PDF to turn it into a PDF.

(4) Earn through programs for residual income

You can earn residuals, or monthly commissions, from many online businesses by referring customers. In contrast to a regular 9–5, you must continue to work in order to be paid, and you are only compensated for your efforts after they are over. You can work once and continue to get paid with residuals. We call this LEVERAGE!

Lets say you write a book as an independent contractor and set up a contract to receive royalties each time a book sells. You completed the work once, but you still get paid. The same is true of leftover programs. It can be a membership site for a product or service that someone buys after clicking on your affiliate link. You once worked and recommended someone. Every single month, you continue to get a portion of their monthly payment. working intelligently rather than hard.

(5) **Profit from Facebook groups**

In your niche, start a free FACEBOOK GROUP. Next, choose a THEME for your group that will keep participants interested. The key is participation and consistency! You must participate in your group on a daily basis and greet guests.

Make a call to action in a pinned post:

1. Utilize this free group to conduct contests, weekly action assignments, webinars, trainings, etc.
2. Produce an information product to complement the free value.
3. Hold a worthwhile webinar and end it with a promotion for your information product. 4. Continue interacting and promoting goods in your niche.

Using the search bar, look up Facebook Groups: (Do the opposite of what everyone else is doing)

1. Inquire about joining
2. Connect, like, and comment on the posts (instead of spamming like everyone else) 3. Deliver worth (blog posts, articles, videos, tips)
4. Request that others rejoin your group.

Facebook groups are a fantastic way to foster a sense of community. People crave the sense of belonging more than anything else. People enjoy moving "with" the other members of their community. It greatly simplifies the process of "selling".

CHAPTER 2

(6) Earn money by speaking with experts

Undoubtedly, this is among the simplest ways to get money. You locate a professional in your field and only get in touch with them to inquire about conducting an interview. You can do your interview using Google Hangout or audio or video. Make a list of inquiries that they can fully respond to in order to give your specialized value. Ask inquiries on forums where people from your niche hang together.

In your interviews, use those queries. That is a product all by itself. People will pay for that expert's knowledge. Simply create a sales page (I use LeadPages) or use the Profits Theme on WordPress. You may also contract it out. Put your goods up for sale after that on jvzoo, warrior, or clickbank. You could even commit to conducting consistent interviews and make it a membership website. You may connect with experts and share their worth without having to be an expert. This increases both their exposure and your reputation.

(7) **Create software with rights for resale**

Do you take programming seriously? Are you tech savvy? Do you have anything and all work is done on computers? If so, you might enjoy the following suggestions:
Create software with rights for resale:
This is a terrific way to get extra money if you are an excellent programmer.

If you can develop a program that meets a client demand, you can sell it for a sizable sum of money because there are so many websites and varied wants.

You might also grant the program resale rights, allowing others to sell it and earn commissions. You are allowed to charge more if you do this. This is ideal if you want to make a lot of money but aren't a great marketer.

Here are some actions you can take in order to sell software:

Prior to building your software, examine the general requirements of the buyer. Excellent research is done into this by OnSellingSoftware.

Find out on forums what your friends or potential customers would most like software for.
In websites or forums, promote your program. Additionally, you can advertise through various traffic strategies, among friends, or on social media.

What kind of profit can I expect from it?

This will depend on the software's complexity and the price you decide to set for it.

(8) **Make money on instagram**

Instagram is a fantastic technique to grab your audience's attention because people are visual creatures. Vibrant, high-quality Instagram photographs help strengthen your brand. Include some value in the form of TIPS in your descriptions along with that.
INCLUDE A CALL TO ACTION IN YOUR BIO AND POST REGULARLY! (3 times daily)
You can hold an auction right there on your page or sell online.
Shout outs from those with significant followings to help others get in front of their audience are even paid for.
Release your CREATIVITY—the sky is the limit! There are countless methods to make money quickly using Instagram! You only need to increase your tribe's size or following in order to monetize. The public will also LOVE you for it.

(9) **Podcasting:**

Podcasting is similar to blogging, but done orally rather than on a computer keyboard. You would reap the same advantages and go about it in the same manner (publish consistent content, etc.). But it's only a means to accommodate those who want to learn by listening as opposed to reading.

You'll need a headphone, a microphone, and software to record your audio if you want to start a podcast.

As with blogging, you may make money with podcasting by promoting other services that pay commissions, placing ads, and using Google AdSense.

Here are some actions you may take to start your podcasting career:

Create a website for your podcasts and record your content there. If you don't already have a recording program, try Audacity, which is free.

Create an MP3 version of your recordings, upload it to your website, and then start sharing it. Obtain a conversion to MP3 format.

Put the MP3 on your website. As often as you can, add material to your website to attract repeat listeners.

Start promoting your website among friends, on social networks, or through other traffic-generating strategies.

(10) **Become a translator**

If you speak another language as a second language, choosing to work as a translator will help you earn money. This is yet another simple method for turning your free time into cash. especially if you are familiar with any of the languages for which there is a great need for translators.

Here are some actions you can take to turn into a Translator:
Through any of the freelance websites, you can get translation tasks.
There are numerous websites that only offer translation services. Through any of those websites, you can express your interest and find work as well.

Find the websites that list all the translation-related jobs.
Become a member of those websites.
You might launch your own website to inform visitors about the translation services you are prepared to provide.

How much can I expect to make working as a translator?

Depending on the demand for the language, you might earn anywhere from $0.01 per word. You can charge a reasonable cost per word if there aren't enough translators available for the language.

CHAPTER 3

(11) Links for sale and purchase:

Many people believe that they need a large number of backlinks pointing at their website in order to achieve higher search engine rankings on Google.

Backlinks are essentially links that lead to another website from those on other people's websites. Google offers precedence for their search engine positions when someone links to another person's website because it communicates to Google that the other person's website is worthy of being linked to.

Many people work hard to increase the number of links pointing to their websites since the higher the search engine placement, the more exposure a business receives.

You can make money by serving as a middleman between those who are eager to sell links and those who are willing to buy them because there are so many individuals who want links.

Here are some actions you can perform in order to buy and sell links:

In the forums of websites that discuss links, you can look for people looking to purchase or sell links.

Learn about the rules for link selling and buying.

Promote only worthwhile links (links that have high Page Rank on Google)

You might also make a website to promote your offerings.

Start promoting your website among friends, on social networks, or in other ways to drive traffic.

What kind of profit can I expect from buying and selling links?

It depends on how much you charge for making introductions. You can even generate your own pricing by purchasing links on your own and charging customers for them. Depending on how good the site is, you might earn anywhere from $1 to $300 for a link.

(12) **Outsourcing middle-man or agent**

Many businesses look to hire someone to help them develop their online presence, to write blog posts, or to help them with other responsibilities.
You might work as a "agent" for some outsourcers if you are skilled at both marketing and people management. Determine who can perform a particular task, and then promote their services to other companies. Increase the price to increase your profit.

Here are some actions you may do to become an outsourcing middleman:
To identify people you can hire, search through websites, forums, and freelance sites.
Create a website where you list the services that your team is capable of doing, along with costs and turnaround times.
Start promoting your website among friends, on social networks, or with other traffic strategies.

Start expanding your clientele. Work hard, put referral programs in place, and begin gathering endorsements from the people you assist.

How much money can I make as a middleman in outsourcing?
How much you can earn mostly relies on the services you provide, the number of clients you can serve at once, and your marketing skills.

(13) **SSL Certificates for sale:**

Websites frequently employ SSL certificates to demonstrate the security of their pages. After users confirm the legitimacy of a secure site, this certificate is digitally "signed" by a certificate authority they already have faith in.

Webmasters NEED the SSL certificates because many website visitors need to know a site is secure before they submit payment or personal information.

Any business that sells SSL certificates might allow you to associate with them and market their products. These businesses will either give you a discount on their SSL certificates so you may resell them, or they will give you rewards based on how many sales you generate. Examples of these incentives can be found here or here.

Here are some actions you can do to join as a partner to resell SSL certificates:

Make a list of the businesses that provide SSL certificates by searching the internet.

Open a partnership account with the business.

Determine potential clients, then close the deal.

Give the business a list of the number of sales you generated for the month.

Enjoy the bonus sales!

What kind of profit can I expect from reselling SSL certificates?

It depends on how many certificates you sell and how much the company that you have joined forces with is willing to offer in sales incentives if they do.

Your profit will be the margin you maintain for yourself if the business you've partnered with offers certificates at a reduced price for you.

(14) Create and sell ClipArt:

If you have graphic design skills, you can create various ClipArt and icons to sell.

Many webmasters are eager to pay for your ideas because they typically need to make their websites look vibrant and welcoming.

You can either create ClipArt to sell to the general public or create unique designs for customers depending on their websites and niches.

More details about producing ClipArt are available right here.

Here are some actions you may take to use clipart to earn money:

(15) **Create a website for you.**

Make a personal portfolio for yourself, then showcase it on your website.
Choose whether to sell your photos individually or in collections.
Promote your business on websites, forums, social media, via friends, or with other traffic-generating strategies.

How much can I expect to earn?

This will depend on whether you want to sell items individually (for as little as $.50 an image or much more), or in packages (which would then depend on sizes of the packages and your reputation in the field).

(16) **Earn through consulting and coaching**

Do you have a talent and a passion for assisting others in achieving their objectives? You can give a sample of what you have to offer through your online brand by using your blog, videos, writing, audios, etc. These can be low-cost or free products that serve as an introduction before you promote coaching services.

Newsletter, articles, and e-books are additional formats for coaching services.
4. Audio/Visual 6. Skype meetings, 5. Webinars.

Focus on a TARGET customer and create a plan for 30 days, 90 days, six months, or a year. For high-quality coaching and consulting services, customers are willing to spend upwards of $10,000. A million dollars is equal to 100 coaching students each paying $10,000 per year. Some of the highest paid online business people are coaches!

CHAPTER 4

(17) **Earn through virtual assistance**

Many business owners are stressed out and in need of assistance. They frequently OUTSOURCE some of their workload online.

The good news is that you may apply online to be a VA if you have experience in ADMIN job but don't want to go back to a typical 9–5 outside the home. You might be ideal for this position if you have strong computer and phone skills and are well organized. You can be required to complete the following TASKS: document preparation, database management, customer service, travel reservations, marketing project management, social media management, etc.

(18) **Engage in compensated or paid surveys:**

Many students enjoy using this method to earn money quickly and easily. When you work with paid surveys, you are compensated for both your participation and opinion. Even if these options don't pay as well as some other ones, the money adds up, and the job is all quite simple.

Here are some actions you can do to engage in paid surveys:

Find reputable sites for paid surveys.

Sign up for a few websites to begin with.

Tell the business about the types of surveys you'd be interested in taking.

Start answering as many surveys as you can.

Share your sincere thoughts about the merchandise.

Send the completed survey form back as soon as possible or before the deadline.

A PC with an internet connection is required.

You must have an opinion about the item.

To complete the survey and submit it on time, you should have some free time.

What kind of money can I make through paid surveys? Depending on the sort of survey and its length, you might earn anywhere from $1 to $100.
In addition to cash, you can take advantage of freebies, coupons for discounts, a lottery, etc.

(19) **Creating a digital scrapbooking template**

Many people like using scrapbooks to keep their priceless memories alive.

Individuals no longer need to utilize traditional photo albums; instead, many people like going online and storing their memories in digital form.

You may run a very enjoyable business if you can generate unique templates for people or even just generally excellent scrapbook templates for the public.

Here are some actions you may take to use scrapbook layouts to earn money:

Create a website for yourself and list the kinds of services you offer.

Promote your business on websites, forums, social media, via friends, or with other traffic-generating strategies.

Sell your templates to start earning money.

How much can I expect to earn?

Scrapbook templates for the general public can be purchased for $5 and higher, or you can create custom ones for customers starting at $20.

(20)**Jobs in editing and proofreading:**

Before they are ready to be published online, articles or reports occasionally need to be edited and proofread.

You can find editing and proofreading work if you are a native speaker or have a strong grasp of the language in which the client needs a document proofread.

Here are some actions you can do to find editing and proofreading jobs:

Sign up for accounts on websites that offer clients editing and proofreading services.

Examine job posts every day, and apply for positions for which you are qualified.

Get a job and start making money.

How much money can I make working as an editor or proofreader?

This task is very important to many individuals, and they will pay for it. You might be paid by the hour or for the article. If you choose the latter, plan to pay at least $5 Mper hour and as much as $20 per hour for it.

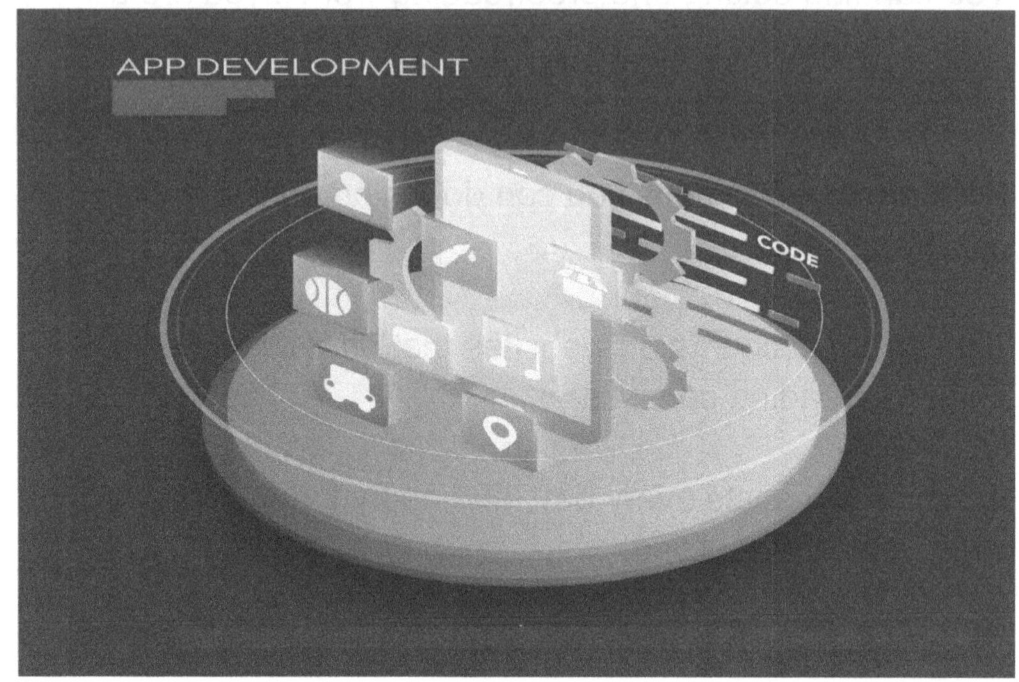

(21) **Create apps**

Everyone has a smartphone, and they all like high-quality applications. Start creating apps if you think you're up for the challenge. You may enter them into the Google or Apple market with a few clicks and begin selling. Look for the most recent trends, then start creating. Overall, developing apps is a low-cost online company that, if done well, may bring in a sizable return. While it could take some effort to get things perfect, applications might ultimately lead to the success you've always desired. Since high-performing apps can generate thousands of dollars in ad revenue each month, this may be a terrific option for you.

CHAPTER 5

(22) Earn from a membership website

a wealth of knowledge to impart? A fantastic approach to create a consistent, long-term income stream is to place your content on a password-protected website and charge your followers a monthly subscription to view it. You can house videos, articles, newsletters, and e-books on your website. You can regularly or weekly contribute to your website. Create live events for your members (Google Hangouts) to keep them interested in your Facebook Group.

You can have a membership site for anything, including a gaming platform, a fitness program, a nutrition program, an earn money program, etc. Discover your niche, provide the content, go out and promote, and you might start accumulating a sizable database of regular paying consumers.

(23) Earn from Fiverr

On Fiverr, you can buy and sell services for $5. Up to $1400 can be offered by sellers as additional gig add-ons for their services. People offer a variety of services, such as voiceovers, social media management, graphic design, any talent, etc., in addition to authoring webpages by hand and taking photos for advertising purposes.

(24)**Take part in contests**:

You might start taking part in contests offered by numerous websites if you have a lot of free time.
Of course, there's a chance you won't take home the prize in every competition, but your chances increase the more you enter.

Little things do add up, and in addition to cash, you may also win prizes like cinema tickets, free samples of goods, gift certificates, etc.
Where can I find competitions?
Make a list of the websites that offer contests after searching the internet.
Become a member of those websites and regularly check for new contests.
Take part in as many competitions as you can

Check the search engines frequently to see if there are any fresh competitions.

What advantages do I get by entering competitions?

Along with other benefits like gift cards, vouchers, and excursions, you can win cash.

(25)**Start an online teaching**:

Start online teaching if you are an expert in any field to earn money.

Any topic may be taught to anyone, anywhere in the world. Online instructors are always needed, especially those from the US and China.

Numerous American students require internet assistance with various tasks, homework, etc.

The demand from Chinese students seeking to learn English is likewise very high.

Teaching people how to use computers online is an additional concept.

Here are some actions you can take in order to begin teaching online:

Create a website for yourself and list the subjects you teach there.

Promote your business on websites, forums, social media, via friends, or with other traffic-generating strategies.

As agreed, give your students the required services. Keep track of the outcomes so you may share them with other potential pupils.

How much money can I expect to make from these jobs?

Depending on your level of experience and subject-matter expertise, you can charge between $4 and $20 per hour.

(26)**Start an online counselling services**

Instead of meeting with counselors in person, many people prefer to use online resources. They believe that by doing this, they can be more anonymous while still enjoying the comfort of not having to drive anywhere.

This could be an enjoyable job for you if you can effectively counsel people. Although it would undoubtedly offer you a competitive edge, you are not required to acquire a specialty degree.

Here are some steps you can take to train as an online counselor:

Make a website outlining your credentials and how you can assist others. Inform individuals if you lack the training or credentials to provide them advice. Some folks may simply offer you money so they can vent their anger while you listen to them. Just be careful not to go beyond what is permitted by law.
Start promoting your website among friends, on social networks, or in other ways to drive traffic.
Start expanding your clientele. Work hard, put referral programs in place, and begin gathering endorsements from the people you assist.

What kind of income can I expect from being an online counselor?

Depending on your level of talent, you can earn up to $200 every hour.

CHAPTER 6

(27) Write articles

You have the option of concentrating completely on writing rather than thinking about the different marketing facets that come with operating an online business. You can earn money for each article you write by contributing to blogs or other websites. E-books and subjects like marketing, law, pharmaceuticals, and other areas that need for specialized expertise will land you higher paying jobs. You can practice as a copywriter, content editor, or both. If you have a knack for writing, you should think about exploring this new career route as freelance writing is becoming more and more popular.

(28) Produce video materials

If you have experience creating video content, you may definitely start a business given the prevalence of video content, especially when it comes to online marketing. Provide potential clients with video packages, hunt for online projects you may join, and most essential, have a strong portfolio. You can make a lot of money with video material, but only if you have the necessary technical know-how and marketing expertise.

(29) **YouTube channel or podcast**

Do you work as a performer? It might be time for you to take the virtual stage and demonstrate your skills. You now have the chance to create a sizable audience and spread your thoughts thanks to the increasing popularity of podcasts and YouTube channels. You may easily make gameplay videos or political commentary with just a few clicks, depending on your intentions. There are those who earned millionaires' fortunes. Thank you to the internet community, so don't be shy about showing off your talent and letting others enjoy it!

(30) **Earn money dropshipping on eBay.**

Ebay is one of the biggest online shopping destinations, and it regularly experiences natural traffic and buyer influxes. Dropping has the advantage of removing the need for physical product storage, inventory management, and transportation. There are no start-up expenses.

Here is how dropshipping works:

Product found on Amazon.com, relisted at a higher price on Ebay, and sold.o Money Transfers To Your Paypal Account Amazon.com Product Purchase Shipment to Customer Direct Revenue I$$
Just visit ebay.com and create a free account there. Find products on other cheap websites, including Walmart.com and Amazon.com, to mention a few. Repost the listing from that website on eBay at a higher cost.
Make sure you have enough money to pay for the product's true cost on the other site, the 17% eBay and PayPal fees, shipping, and yet have some profit left over!
The secret to success is to include all the keywords that consumers would use to find your stuff online in the title!
Once you start putting products up that sell, it becomes a highly passive cash stream because it only takes a few clicks to order from Amazon.com, ship to the buyer, and repost an item when it sells.

This takes some time to get rolling, like everything else. However, with eBay, your things will be discovered by natural traffic. Just keep listing, and soon the sales will flow!

(31) **Build your e - mail list to make money**

One of the best ways to establish a long-lasting online business is through email collection. Your email list becomes an asset for your business. Sales become easier when you establish rapport with your list and customers begin to know, like, and trust you. By sending one straightforward email with a product offer each day, you can make money (affiliate link).
Where do you first of all get your emails from? You must create opt-in pages and provide visitors a reason to enter their email addresses. In return, give them something. Free freebie, intriguing headline that piques readers' interest and leaves them wanting more. through a blog or a capture page

A minimalist website with simply an eye-catching headline and opt-in box is known as a capture page. You can create your capture page using this FREE resource, MITS Pages. Use the capture page link wherever your target audience is, such as in video marketing's description box, article marketing in the signature, social media, solo advertisements, etc. To collect emails into your Aweber account, follow this link (where you store your emails)

CHAPTER 7

(32) **Share your knowledge**

Online learning has reached a new level because to webinars. If you are an authority on a subject, you may share your knowledge online and earn extra money when you're not working. There are several online platforms that provide courses on a range of subjects and allow professionals to sign up as online instructors. You can quickly develop a new interest and source of income if you commit a few hours each week to sharing your views.

(33) **Sell professional photos**

The era of stock photos is gradually coming to an end as online designs strive to use distinctive, high-quality images. If you are an enthusiastic photographer, there are several ways to sell your images online. Publishing high-quality content online will provide you a fantastic chance to make money, and if you also work on building your brand, your chances of making even more money increase.

(34) **Your website space for sale**

You can collaborate with advertisers and sell a section of your page if you already have a blog or website. In this method, each time an advertisement on your website is clicked, you can make money. The CPC (cost-per-click) model is dependent on both the CTR and the volume of traffic to your website (click-through-rate). By using Google AdSense and SEO technologies, you can increase your profit even more. There are many additional tools that can help you make the most of your advertising potential and benefit greatly.

(35) **Forex and stock**

Although the stock and FX markets are seen as dangerous investments, there are many success tales online. If you have prior experience, this could be an excellent chance for you to launch your own internet business. You can make a sizable profit by trading equities and foreign currencies, but it is always preferable to start out small.

(36) **Acquiring online affiliates**

Being an online affiliate may be your best option if you want to make some extra money online without creating any of the products you promote. The majority of the larger businesses, such Amazon, Ebay, and others, have affiliate programs where all you have to do is send traffic to their websites so that people will buy their goods. You will receive a sizeable fee for each sale, with the highest commission rate being somewhere about 8.5%. Users that sign up via your recommendation will also bring you money. You have two options: either create a brand-new website just for a given product type, or include referral links on your current blog or website.

CHAPTER 8

(37) Making Wordpress themes

If you have a knack for website design, another choice is to make your own WordPress themes and sell them. WordPress themes are quite well-liked as a result of the large number of people searching for quick and easy ways to create an online presence. You can make money off of your labor of love by selling your own designs on various websites.

(38) Make money from homemade crafts

Online shoppers have a high demand for handmade goods. Give your imagination free rein. Make sure you can produce it effectively and cheaply. You can even purchase stuff from consignment shops.

After that, you can sell your products on eBay or Etsy.com. Get qualified! Create a personalized banner. Develop your brand with articles, blogs, videos, and other online income opportunities, and before you realize it, you can be a well-known name all over the world.

You name it: headbands, jewelry, bags, scarves, lotions, candles, and so much more! You may sell whatever you make online!

(39) **Get a part-time employment in data entry:**

Many businesses receive sporadic requests for various things, like changing hard copy data to electronic data.

Why not earn money if you have excellent accuracy and keyboarding abilities?

Here are some measures you can take to become a part-time data entry operator.
Apply for those positions now.
Finish the paperwork on time.
Do the job as accurately as feasible
Return the assignment within the allotted time.

Gather endorsements and provide rewards to encourage people to recommend their friends.

What is the potential income from data entry?
Depending on how quickly you work and how challenging the job is, you might earn anywhere from $1 to $5 per hour.

(40) **Create websites**

Offering a website building service can make you a lot of money if you enjoy coding. Create your own website and list your services there. Start a marketing campaign and promote your service on social media. To draw in as many clients as you can, pay attention to current trends and follow them. You will need to learn new things frequently because the field of web design is continually evolving. A quick Google search will give you an overview of the most recent design trends.

(41) **Expert in social media**

Due to social media's rising popularity, big businesses require experts who can simultaneously handle several social media accounts. Look for opportunities to work as a social media expert or consultant, and be ready to implement or, in some situations, even design a social media marketing strategy for the business. If you have work experience and understand how to convert social media connections into clients, that's great!

CHAPTER 9

(42) **Earn cash through Google Hangouts**

Google Hangouts and other live events are effective ways to CONNECT with your audience in real time. While video is a fantastic method to interact, being in person fosters a stronger sense of know, like, and trust. Questions from your audience can be answered RIGHT NOW. People are more likely to take action when bonuses and limited-time special offers are made available.

Structure of Live Events:

1. Describe the lessons they will learn.
2. Share your experience, from adversity to success
3. Offer assistance and instruction (the what)
4. Provide testimonies
5. State a dilemma
6. 6. Offer the answer.
7. Conclude with a time-sensitive offer (the how) 8. Ask inquiries (interactive Q&A)

Through LIVE EVENTS such as online Google Hangouts, I have made thousands of dollars. You should be able to earn six figures online pretty quickly if you can master webinars. Make it a point to start participating in other people's online webinars and paying attention to the steps they guide you through. The best approach to LEARN is in this way! Study those who are successful.

(43)**Earn money from free sites**

You'll enjoy making money with freebie sites if you enjoy experimenting with different goods and services. Fortune 500 organizations actually PAY certain businesses by giving their services a trial period to discover them NEW prospective CUSTOMERS.
You register for an account and search for different things you want to try. A minor fee of $1–$5 is sometimes required, sometimes it's free for 30 days, and other times it's only the cost of shipping, etc.

(44)**Get into the Dormain industry**

Even though you might believe that the best deals have already been made for domains, this is not the case.

As it just involves a minimal investment, many people buy and sell domain names to make money.

You can get a good notion of the most popular domain names right now by doing some comprehensive research.

This will enable you to purchase potential domain names that can then be sold for a profit in the future.

Look for domain auction sites online so you can come across expired names that have returned to the pool and are for sale.

The chances are high, that\syou will be the next domain guru, who can make a huge profit.

(45) **Create a product of your own, then start selling it online**

You can start selling your creations online and earn money if you have a talent for something like knitting your own sweater, painting, making decorative items, etc.

Where can I buy things to sell?

Register on websites like Etsy, Amazon, and eBay.

Describe your products

Sell your goods and begin to profit.

How much can I expect to earn?

It depends on the product's nature and your pricing policy.

CHAPTER 10

(46) **Engage in online research:**

Internet research and data collection are constantly needed because new enterprises are starting up every day.

This manifests in numerous ways. For instance, the necessary information and provide a report for them. This report will be used to help them decide whether they should even start the firm.

There are various additional research positions available, and they can be a lot of fun to learn about.
The findings of the research will determine whether or not to launch the firm. If you are internet savvy and have a lot of free time, it is a smart idea to take on online research jobs given the necessity for the position.

Here are some actions you may take to earn money conducting research online:

Search for online research positions.

Conduct extensive investigation and present the customer with a report as requested.

How much can I earn from these research jobs?

Depending on the difficulty and extent of the required research, fixed price jobs might pay anywhere from $5 to $200.

Depending on your experience, you can charge anything between $3 and $50 per hour if you work hourly employment.

(47)**Provide services for video montage:**

Another service where you may provide assistance in people's memory-making is this one.

You can run a successful and enjoyable business if you can take some photos that a customer supplies, create a beautiful slide show with background music, and burn it to DVD.

These video montages would be wonderful one-of-a-kind gifts for folks that would last a lifetime.

You will probably generate more revenue if you are more creative. Check this this to see how some individuals advertise their montages.

Here are some actions you can take to earn money using video montage services:

Build a personal website.

Post some illustrations of video montages.

Inform your loved ones about your new service.

Promote your business on websites, forums, social media, via friends, or with other traffic-generating strategies.

How much can I expect to earn?

The price range for a montage is $20 to $200.

(48) **Start your eCommerce career**

You can quickly set up your own online store using Shopify and Woocommerce. If you already have a product in mind, you can start selling it online with ease. You can also use various methods, such as dropshipping, to avoid headaches associated with product storage or delivery.

(49) **Become an expert in online marketing**

Do you have any SEO expertise? Are you familiar with SEM? You are currently pursuing a career in web marketing. When a website has rock-star content and has been optimized for SEO, it is time for the SEM (Search Engine Marketing). The likelihood that you can launch an internet business is significant if you have expertise and expert knowledge of online marketing strategies. Since businesses typically outsource these tasks, there is a sizable market of potential clients. And a fantastic opportunity to make a significant profit!

(50) **Create a blog**

Even though it appears to be hard in this day and age to make money blogging, many people have succeeded in doing so. Giving blogging a go is possible if you are motivated and have a strong desire to write. It doesn't take much technical knowledge to set up your own blog, but obtaining lots of traffic is another story. Choosing a topic is never easy. If you have expertise in something, you might decide to share it with others so that other professionals might benefit. You will need to put in time to develop a solid following, regardless of your topic. You can then market other brands, establish new business contacts, and eventually make money thanks to this.
Even though blogging is somewhat cutthroat, if you have a way with words, you can succeed financially.

Useful sites to help you achieve your financial freedom

1. Blogging
   (www.yourpassion.com)
2. Buying and selling links
   (http://www.linkadage.com)
3. Freelancing:
   -Data entry job
   -Visual assistant job
   -Editing and proofreading
   -Email and phone handling
   -Design and build websites for people
   -Design banners, logos
   -SEO optimized articles etc
   (www.lance.com)
   (www.guru.com)
   (www.odesk.com)
4. Applications tester
   (www.I shir.com/independent- application-testing. htm)
5. Design website for yourself
   (http://www.phpbbhs.com/index.HTML)
6. Make money with misspellings
   (Namecheap.com)
7. Buy or sell websites
   (www.websitebroker.com)
   (Flippa.com)
8. Online shopping
   (Amazon.com)
   (eBay.com)
9. EBook publishing

(Amazon kdp.com)

10. Teaching online
    (http://www.e-tutor.com)
    (http://www.live-tutor.com)
11. Software design and review services
    (http://www.softwarejudge.com)
    (http://philip.greenspun.com)
12. Telecommunication jobs
    (http://www.tjobs.com)
13. Flipping domains
    (Business.com)
    (www.namepros.com)
    (http//:www.dnforum.com)
14. Get paid to read emails
    (http://www.getpaid5times.com)
    (http://wowearnings.com)

15. Transcription services
    (http://www.way with words.eu)
16. Expert guide
    (About.com)
17. Affiliate marketing progprogram
    (Clickbank.com)
    (Jvzoo.com)
    (Warriorplus.com)
18. Google AdSense
    (WordPress.com)
19. Hosting
    (Hostgator.com)
20. Classified advertising
    (craigstlist.com)

Conclusion

I hope you have liked reading this ebook and that it has given you many ideas about how to earn money online. All you have to do is act!
IDEA + ACTION = INCOME
ADVICE + ACTION = PROFIT

I made an effort to identify various income streams for all types of people, and I genuinely hope that some of these spoke to you.

Keep in mind that you are free to combine these techniques. Even while some of them don't bring in as much money, they're still enjoyable and a good addition to your repertoire.

Anyone who aspires to financial independence should take this book very seriously.

Thank you once more for reading. Please go through the book to learn about some of the best ways you can support your goals.

I Wish You Success!

Ibe Okechukwu

About The Author

Ibe Okechukwu has been earning online passive income since 2017.

He is an educationist and a theologian by training who has worked in several reputable financial and educational establishments for over two decades.

He has organized several seminars and workshop trainings and also been invited as guest speaker to several news broadcasts and presentations on radio and television.

He counts being an author, teacher, farmer, soap and skincare formulator and a lefthanders' advocate. He also works with non - profits and currently the Director of Extra Miles Consult.

www.ingramcontent.com/pod-product-compliance
Lightning Source LLC
LaVergne TN
LVHW050011170826
845677LV00023B/3854

* 9 7 9 8 3 7 2 9 6 4 9 3 8 *